Land of Milk and Honey

Land of Milk and Honey

Travels in the History of Indian Food

CHITRITA BANERJI

LONDON NEW YORK CALCUTTA

Seagull Books

Editorial offices:

1st Floor, Angel Court, 81 St Clements Street
Oxford OX4 1AW, UK

1 Washington Square Village, Apt 1U, New York
NY 10012, USA

26 Circus Avenue, Calcutta 700 017, India

'Food, Ritual and Art in Bengal' and 'How Bengal Discovered *Chhana*' were originally presented at the Oxford Symposium on Food and Cookery in 1998 and 1999, respectively. A slightly different version of 'The Propitiatory Meal' was first published in *Gastronomica*, *The Journal of Food and Culture* (Winter 2003).

All illustrations in this volume are from Ashit Paul (ed.), *Woodcut Prints of Nineteenth Century Calcutta* (Seagull Books, 1983).

ISBN-10 1 9054 2 234 2
ISBN-13 978 1 905422 34 0

British Library Cataloguing-in-Publication Data
A catalogue record for this book is available from the British Library

Typeset by Seagull Books, Calcutta, India
Printed in the United Kingdom by Biddles Ltd, King's Lynn

Contents

How Bengal Discovered Chhana

ASK ANY INDIAN and you will be told that Bengal excels in the taste and variety of its milk-based sweets. Of these, the sweets made from *chhana* (cottage cheese or acid-curd cheese) are unique to the region. Nowhere else in India does the confectioner work such magic through manipulating this substance which is derived by cutting milk with acid. And since vegetarians as well as fish- and meat-eaters relish sweets, Bengal's *chhana*-based concoctions have long been famed outside the region. Two sweets, in particular, *sandesh* and *rosogolla*, are practically synonymous with the sweet-toothed Bengali, with his longstanding reputation as an indolent, easygoing, comfort-loving gourmet.

But what is the reason for the pre-eminence of *chhana* in this eastern corner of the Indian subcontinent? And why is it not associated with sweet-making in the rest of the country? The answer lies in an encounter between two races—historic, yet forgotten by most Bengalis today. It began five hundred years ago, when the Portuguese explorer, Vasco da Gama, landed on the western coast of India in 1498. To fully realize its significance, we need to understand the long-held beliefs about the nature of milk that prevailed among the people of this region.

Just as in medieval European physiology, the four humours—blood, phlegm, choler and bile—were thought to be the constituents of the human body, their respective proportions determining an individual's character, mood and health, similarly, in the ancient Indian system of Ayurveda, the body is dominated by one of three elements—*sattva*, *raujas* and *taumas*—each imparting specific characteristics. And extending the notion that we are what we eat, the ancients ascribed those same characteristics to different foods. In this hierarchical universe, milk (including its derivatives, *ghee*, buttermilk, cream, yogurt) is easily in the top bracket. It is the purest of edibles whose quality is *sattvika* (descriptive form of *sattva*): nutritive, agreeable, conducive to serenity and spirituality. Sages and ascetics, who left all worldly ties behind and isolated themselves in the wilderness in search of higher metaphysical truths, subsisted on milk provided by local devotees. Milk was the one food that would not induce worldly desires or distractions in their minds. This belief in the semi-sacred quality of milk is also reflected in its consistent use as an offering to the gods. Rice pudding, for instance, is one of the commonest items offered to important household deities like Lakshmi, the goddess of wealth and prosperity. Even outside of Hinduism, milk retains its connotation of purity. The first food with which the Buddha broke his long fast after achieving Nirvana was milk-based.

A famous turn-of-the century Bengali food writer, Bipradas Mukhopadhyay, in his 1906 book, *Mishtanno Pak* (Making Sweets), documents the different types of milk and their specific qualities as set down by the ancients. Starting with the milk of cows, goats and ewes, the list goes on to enumerate water buffaloes, camels, mares, female elephants and women as acceptable sources of milk for human consumption. Cow's milk, as one would expect, is defined as second only to human milk in its wide-ranging benefits. Whatever the source, all milk was believed to have several properties in common: tasty, soothing, energizing, cool, rich, sperm-generating, reducing bile and gout and conducive to phlegm.

Milk was also an important part of the diet of ordinary people. Unlike the ascetic, the householder looked on milk with infinite desire. It was not only health food par excellence, it had powerful symbolic value as an image of achievable prosperity. In agriculture-based Bengal, 'milk-and-rice' became synonymous with the sustenance of a comfortable life. Vegetarians and non-vegetarians alike considered milk a precious food. Both the folktales as well as the substantial body of orally transmitted ditties (*chharas*) of Bengal are replete with images of milk that connote plenty and prosperity. Kings are anointed with milk and butter before their coronation. Princesses bathe in copiously flowing milk. Young girls hope to improve their complexion by washing their faces with milk. Mothers who suddenly encounter lost children after many years find their breasts spouting milk. Rivers of milk, rippling waves of milk, lakes of milk, trembling layers of thickened milk, even oceans of milk recur with amazing frequency in myths, folktales, poems and songs.

A famous Bengali folktale, recounting the adventures of two young princes named Sheet and Basanta (also the words for Winter and Spring, respectively), demonstrates the extraordinarily vivid presence of milk in the folk imagination. Separated from his older brother Sheet, Basanta was discovered in the woods by a holy man who raised him as his disciple. One day, sitting under a tree, Basanta heard two parrots talking to each other about a fabulous gem that the king of the elephants carried on his head. Anyone who got hold of it would be able to marry the beautiful princess Rupabati. Immediately, Basanta decided to set off in search of this gem. After travelling for twelve years and thirteen days, he reached the realm of the royal elephant. But a huge, white mountain barred the way. Down its body flowed cascades of milk; its peak was smothered in quivering layers of *sar* (the thick skin skimmed off from the top as heated milk cools down). Basanta climbed to the top and saw on the other side an expansive ocean filled with thick, rich milk. In that ocean bloomed thousands of fragrant golden lotuses and in their midst frolicked a beautiful, milk-white elephant, on whose head glowed a gem that seemed brighter than all the jewels of the world put together.

But as soon as Basanta jumped into the ocean of milk, it became a sandy desert.

An ancient tale from the Mahabharata describes how the gods and demons got together to churn the ocean of milk in the hope of obtaining ambrosia which would make them immortal. But after hauling up many wondrous treasures—including the sacred pitcher of ambrosia—a virulent poison, distilled from the venom of all the serpents who ruled the underworld, rose to the surface. And immediately, the ocean of milk was transformed into the expanse of salt water that we mortals know today.

Both these stories illustrate a deep conviction about the fragility of milk. The introduction of an alien element destroys the very nature of the life-giving, life-sustaining fluid. Deliberately doing so, could, therefore, easily be deemed sacrilegious. For many centuries, the importance of that belief was instrumental in limiting the people of Bengal (as well as of the rest of India) in the uses they found for milk and the products they derived from it.

The use of milk and the general beliefs about its properties continued unchanged into the medieval period, as can be seen from literary evidence. Medieval Bengali literature abounds in long narrative poems. Some of them are full of descriptions of food that highlight the connection between human temperament and the nature of food and here, too, milk and its derivatives—*ghee*, yogurt or buttermilk—exemplify the nobler qualities. In the sixteenth-century *Chandimangalkabya*, written by Mukundaram Chakrabarti, descriptions of meals include those prepared for Shiva and Vishnu. Shiva, who is considered choleric and prone to violence, eats food cooked with pungent mustard oil, not *ghee*. Vishnu, on the other hand, is imagined as having a serene temperament and is offered *sattvika* foods including tender vegetables cooked in *ghee* and a variety of desserts, all derived from milk.

These medieval poems refer to many desserts that followed elaborate meals, and milk was the basis for quite a few. Rice pudding—called *paramanno*, meaning the ultimate rice or best rice, in both Sanskrit and Bengali—was not only offered to the gods but was also a human favourite. It was a feature of most festive meals and many secular rituals. So was sweetened yogurt, which (along with its unsweetened version) had highly auspicious connotations. But the commonest material for making sweets was *kheer*, that is, milk which has been boiled down and reduced until it is either a thick, viscous liquid (similar to what is sold as evaporated milk in Western supermarkets), or a tight, slightly grainy solid. This latter version is often called *khoa kheer* and has the virtue of remaining unspoiled much longer than any other form of milk, an important consideration in a humid, tropical climate.

The evidence is bolstered by another famous medieval work of literature, neither mythic nor fictional, but a biography in narrative verse. *Chaitanyacharitamrita* by Krishnadas Kabiraj recounts the life and times of the remarkable religious reformer known as Sri Chaitanya. Born into an orthodox Hindu brahman family of Vedic scholars, Chaitanya rejected the strict hierarchy and cruel discrimination of the Hindu caste system. He preached a message of equality, brotherhood, love and non-violence. The oppressed members of the lower castes followed him in droves and emulated his personal habits, which included strict vegetarianism, a practice not common until then—even among brahmans—in fish-loving Bengal.

The importance of this biography to historians of Bengali food is immeasurable. When barely out of his teens, Krishnadas Kabiraj became a devout follower of Chaitanya. The latter took him everywhere he went, including the homes of other wealthy disciples. This provided Krishnadas with an intimate knowledge of every aspect of Chaitanya's daily life. In the biography, he describes in fascinating detail the numerous elaborate vegetarian meals prepared for Chaitanya in the

How Bengal Discovered Chhana

Chaitanya, as an incarnation of Rama and Krishna, along with disciples.

homes of admirers. A staggering variety of sweets are mentioned, indicating that despite his abjuration of human intimacy and worldly possessions, Chaitanya had a Bengali predilection for sweets. Many of these were made with puffed, popped or flaked rice, combined with white or brown sugar and/or *kheer*. Others were concocted from flour, coconut, ground legumes or sesame seeds. Krishnadas also mentions an impressive array of purely milk-based sweets—*kheer* mixed with sliced mangos, sweetened yogurt and items like *dugdha-laklaki*, *sarbhaja*, *sarpupee* and *sandesh*.

For those unfamiliar with Bengali food, some explanation of these terms is required in order to appreciate the point made earlier, the taboo on making a deliberate, invasive change to the nature of milk which, clearly, still prevailed at this time. Three of the sweets served to Chaitanya—*dugdha-laklaki* (known today as *raabri*), *sarbhaja* and *sarpupee* (known today as *sarpuria*)—are mutations of *sar*, which is as precious to the people of the Indian subcontinent as cream is to the West. In a tropical region, before the advent of refrigeration, the only way to preserve milk (without making it into *kheer*) was to repeatedly boil it, the notion of pasteurization being still far into the future. A by-product of all this boiling was the transformation of the fatty top layer into a 'skin'. Each time the milk came to a boil, a new skin would form and it would be skimmed off, added to the previous layers and pressed together. These thick layers were used to make *sar*-based sweets. *Dugdha-laklaki* is layers of *sar* cut into squares and floating in mildly sweetened milk, sometimes flavoured with saffron. *Sar* fried in *ghee* and soaked in syrup becomes *sarbhaja*. Fried in *ghee*, layered with crushed almonds, *khoa kheer* and cardamom, and then soaked in sweetened milk, it becomes *sarpuria*. As for *the sandesh* mentioned by Krishnadas Kabiraj and other contemporary writers, it was sweetened pellets of *khoa kheer*.

What is notable in all these descriptions is that not a single sweet is made from *chhana*. Modern food historians like K. T. Achaya have discussed the Aryan taboo on cutting milk with acid. It is notable that in all the myths about the young Krishna, who was brought up by foster parents among the milkmen of Brindaban (in the state of Uttar Pradesh), there are thousands of references to milk, butter, *ghee* and yogurt but none to *chhana*. Even now, the practice of adding acid to make cheese is not to be seen in northern India. Sweets offered in the temples of modern Brindaban (sacred to Krishna worshippers) are invariably made of solidified *kheer*. In making sweets from milk, Chaitanya's medieval contemporaries were,

Chitrita Banerji

Episode from the life of Krishna:
Dadhimanthan (Churning of Curd).

therefore, adhering to the tradition prevalent throughout the Indian subcontinent at that point in time.

And yet, as noted earlier, whenever Bengali sweets are mentioned today, it is the *chhana*-based confections that everyone thinks of. The introduction of *chhana* into the Bengali—indeed, Indian—food universe in the centuries following Chaitanya, and its enthusiastic adoption, remains a wonderful metaphor for the enrichment of societies through encounters with the unknown.

Enter the Portuguese. From Portugal to Bengal is a distance not only of several thousand miles, but also of climate, topography and terrain. The connection between the two is neither obvious nor memorable. Britain, not Portugal, France or Holland, became the dominant colonial power in India once the East India Company had cemented its hold over Bengal following a decisive victory in the 1757 Battle of Plassey. Traders and fortune-hunters from these other European countries, however, had been coming to India long before the establishment of British control. Some formed small settlements that bear their imprint to this day—the Portuguese enclave of Goa on the western coast of India and the French enclaves of Chandannagar and Pondicherry on the east. But it was a Portuguese settlement in Bengal, so hazy in the regional memory, which made a revolutionary contribution to the region's food universe, as can be seen from trawling the byways of the past.

Although Portugal does not head the list of European countries in terms of gourmet cheeses, it does have several unique varieties. In the introduction to her book, *The Food of Spain and Portugal*, Elisabeth Lambert Ortiz talks about their excellence. Most are made of sheep or goat's milk, but cow's milk is also used. She describes the innumerable fresh cheeses, *queijos frescos*, made into little cakes about three inches in diameter. When mature, they are firm, with a strong flavour. When fresh, they are soft and spreadable. The importance of *queijos frescos* in the Portuguese diet is demonstrated by the migration of the product. This cheese can be found in the refrigerated food section of many speciality shops in American cities with large Portuguese communities.

Shift the scene to modern Bengal. One of the curiosities available in Calcutta's New Market (Hogg Market in the early days of British colonialism) is 'bandel cheese'. It comes in the form of little cakes of fresh cow's milk cheese, remarkably similar to the kind mentioned by Elisabeth Lambert Ortiz. But ask the shopkeepers why the cheese is called 'bandel' or what its origins are, and they are likely to be stumped.

Certainly most people buying the cheese are not aware of any possible connection between this product and the Portuguese traders who followed Vasco da Gama and settled in large numbers in Bengal during the sixteenth and seventeenth centuries. Nor does the average consumer realize that the numerous sweets made from *chhana* that s/he loves are, in a sense, the siblings or cousins of this same 'bandel cheese.'

But each time the Bengali rolls his or her tongue around the spongy juiciness of a *rosogolla*, or revels in the delicate graininess of a *sandesh*, the forgotten encounter between two races comes to life. For the Portuguese not only contributed the comparatively obscure 'bandel cheese' to the gourmet Bengali's platter, their distinctive way of processing milk also initiated a whole new flowering of the Bengali culinary imagination.

The advent of European traders permanently changed many aspects of eating in the Indian subcontinent. Not only was it a case of East meeting West in terms of diet and cookery, it also meant a significant enlargement of the subcontinent's food repertoire. For the Europeans, who came in search of Eastern spices, brought with them the vegetables they had discovered in the New World. The earliest and foremost traders were, of course, the Portuguese who discovered the direct sea route from Europe to Asia. For almost the entire sixteenth century, Portugal virtually monopolized this route.

During that time, they spread their area of operations along both coasts of India. In the east, they settled in large numbers in Bengal, along the Hooghly river. Initially, they had a fearsome reputation in Bengal, since some of them used their navigational skills to commit daring acts of piracy along the coast as well as in the interior where the numerous rivers served as primary conduits for goods and passengers. Many of the Portuguese also intermarried with the locals, thus paving the way for a more intimate exchange between the two races. Among the new crops they introduced were tobacco, potato, cashew, papaya, guava and a host of vegetables.

Modern compendiums on the cheeses of the world stress the paucity of cheeses in the cuisine of Asia, a fact attributed to the humid tropical climate, which made it difficult to apply the sophisticated preservation techniques needed for the famous cheeses of Europe. Among the few cheeses found in the Indian subcontinent today are the ubiquitous *paneer* (familiar to Westerners through the good offices of Indian restaurants serving dishes like *matar-paneer* and *saag-paneer*), a couple of varieties from Gujarat and two from Bengal.

How Bengal Discovered Chhana

Books like Sandy Carr's *Simon and Schuster Pocket Guide to Cheese* and Geoffrey Campbell-Platt's *Fermented Foods of the World* refer to the two cheeses of Bengal as *chhana* and *bandal*. Both are described as 'acid-curd cheeses' made from cow or buffalo milk, although no mention is made of how they came into being.

Bandal, however, is pronounced *bandel* in Bengali and a little digging reveals that it is cheese that is made only in Bandel, a town situated twenty-five miles north of Calcutta on the banks of the Hooghly. The name derives from the Bengali term *bandar*, meaning port. The Portuguese had originally chosen the nearby town of Hooghly (which they called Ugolim) as their centre of operations. But in 1632 they suffered a serious defeat at the hands of the imperial Mughal army. They then retreated to Bandel, which was, at the time, the chief port on the Hooghly, and formed a second, more lasting establishment. The reason for Bandel's continued popularity as a settlement, among not only the Portuguese but also other Europeans, was its supposed salubrious qualities. Many of them went there to convalesce and recover from the trying effects of the local climate. A report in the *Calcutta Gazette* of 3 September 1799, for example, says, 'Sir Robert Chambers, Judge of the Supreme Court, had gone to spend the vacation at the pleasant and healthy settlement of Bandel.'

Today, the chief relic of this flourishing Portuguese colony is the Bandel Church, the oldest Christian church in Bengal. The present structure, according to some historians, replaced an older one built by the Portuguese in their fort in 1599, which was razed to the ground by the Mughal army on the capture of the town in 1632. The present church and monastery are said to have been built in 1660 by Gomez de Soto, who had managed to save the keystone of the old church, bearing the date 1599, during the sack of the town.

K. T. Achaya documents the establishment of the Portuguese community in Bengal: By the second half of the seventeenth century, they [the Portuguese settlers] numbered 20,000 with some at Rajmahal. 'They loved cottage cheese, which they made by "breaking" milk with acidic materials. This routine technique may have lifted the Aryan taboo on deliberate milk curdling and given the traditional Bengali *moira* [confectioner] a new raw material to work with.'

Given this well-established presence, the influence of Portuguese cooking techniques on the eating habits of Bengal is not surprising. It was noted by at least one contemporary travel writer. Francois Bernier, a French doctor, spent seven years in India from 1659 to 1666. He mentions in detail the physical beauty of Bengal and its lush plenitude of grains, vegetables, fish and meat.

He also notes: 'Bengal likewise is celebrated for its sweetmeats, especially in places inhabited by the Portuguese, who are skilful in the art of preparing them and with whom they are an article of considerable trade.'

Although *bandal* (or *bandel*) cheese is now associated with West Bengal (and found only in a few speciality shops), the process of making acid-curd cheeses found another incarnation across the border in the eastern part of Bengal—the famous Dhakai *paneer*. Dhaka, the capital of modern Bangladesh, was known as Rajmahal during the sixteenth and seventeenth centuries when the Portuguese began settling in Bengal. Dhakai *paneer*, as described in the *Simon and Schuster Pocket Guide to Cheese*, is made from cow or buffalo milk, or a mixture of the two. It is drained in wicker or bamboo baskets, pressed and dried for about two weeks, before being smoked. Wedges of salt, placed in the middle, help preserve it and lend sharpness to the taste. The cheese is eaten plain, or sliced and fried gently in clarified butter, or even added to legume and vegetable dishes. Both Dhakai *paneer* and *bandel* cheese, however, remain speciality products and not common items for regular consumption in any part of Bengal.

Neither, however, can be made without curdling milk with acid. It is the solid separated by curdling, that the Bengalis called *chhana*, which has found such wide application in Bengali sweet production and left an entire region indebted to the Portuguese. The etymology of the term is rather obscure but, according to several major Bengali dictionaries, it is a case of a verb becoming a noun. *Chhana* is related to another verb, *shana*. Both mean kneading vigorously by hand to create a fine paste or dough. The naming of *chhana* seems based on the fact that all *chhana*-based sweets require the curdled milk solid to be first kneaded. In fact, the excellence of many sweets depends on the right degree of kneading and often the reputation or status of a Bengali *moira* depended on his success in achieving the right consistency of kneaded *chhana* respective to the sweet being made from it. It is also of interest that the word *chhana* has a separate meaning in colloquial Bengali—children or offspring. And if one considers curdled milk to be the 'offspring' of untreated milk, then this is indeed a serendipitous example of *double entendre*.

In one of the stories of *The Book of Thousand Nights and One Night*, a beautiful female slave called Sympathy the Learned is brought to the court of the Khalifa Harun-al-Rashid and quizzed by a series of scholars and wise men on different branches of knowledge. In answering the questions of a doctor about the treatment and prevention of disease, Sympathy says that gluttony is the cause of all disease. To avoid gluttony, one has to divide the belly into three parts, one to be filled with food, one with water, and one with nothing at all so that the body has room to breathe and the soul can lodge comfortably.

Whatever one may think of the efficacy of this charming formulation (which is not so far from modern directives of health), the image of the Bengali *moira* is that of a man at the other end of the spectrum. A mountainous figure with a ballooning middle, he gives the impression that all three parts of his belly are more than full. He is a famously sedentary character, sitting all day in front of his stove, surrounded by huge containers filled with *chhana* and *kheer* from which he concocts the infinite variety of sweets that are synonymous with gourmet eating in Bengal. Clad only in the traditional white dhoti from the waist down, he leaves his torso bare except for a red and white checked *gaamchha* (napkin) flung over one shoulder and used frequently to mop his sweating face and neck. The aphorism about the *moira* never eating *sandesh* is supposed to indicate a gluttony that has resulted in absolute satiety.

It should be noted that the *sandesh* today is a totally different creation from the one offered to Chaitanya and his medieval contemporaries. The latter, as mentioned above, was made from sweetened, solidified *kheer*. Since the dryness of the *kheer* made it easy to preserve, Bengalis developed the custom of carrying some *sandesh* with them whenever they visited someone. The term *sandesh* also meant news, and the sweet, therefore, became the perfect offering for a visitor bearing news or interested in getting the host's news.

Chhana has different consistencies. As Achaya notes, 'mild precipitation of milk using whey yields a soft but perishable *chhana* product, while the use of lime juice yields a gritty one which sets to a hard, long-lasting product.' It is hard to determine exactly when the term *sandesh* came to indicate a sweet made with *chhana* rather than with *kheer*. But it is reasonable to assume that it had become common usage by the latter half of the nineteenth century. Today, the simplest Bengali *sandesh* is the *kanchagolla* (literally, 'uncooked ball'), that is, hot, sweetened *chhana* formed into round balls. The term *kancha* (uncooked) does not indicate a lack of processing by heat after the milk has been curdled. The *chhana* is actually tossed lightly with sugar over low heat and the mastery of a *moira* is indicated by the complexity of texture he can achieve despite the shortness of the cooking/processing time. Some of the best *kanchagolla* is available from sweet shops around the famous Kali temple in Calcutta's Kalighat neighbourhood. They are generally given as offerings to the goddess. Once they have gone through the ritual of offering, the devotees are free to eat and enjoy these soft yet grainy rounded shapes served on disposable plates of *shaal* leaves, their milky

The Goddess Kali of Kalighat.

flavour curiously enhanced by the slightly smoky odour of the leaf container.

In more elaborate incarnations, the *chhana* for *sandesh* can be pressed, dried, flavoured with fruit essences, coloured, cooked to many different consistencies, filled with syrup, blended with coconut or *kheer* and moulded into a variety of shapes (including those of elephants, conch shells and tigers). Fancy confectioners in Calcutta or Dhaka even take proprietary pride in a particular shape or flavour of *sandesh* as their particular invention. The Bengali obsession with this sweet is indicated in the flights of fancy displayed in the naming of different kinds of *sandesh*. Bipradas Mukhopadhyay, writing in 1906, lists more than twenty names, based on form, content, consistency and flavour. Among the most memorable are: *abaar khabo* (I want to eat it again), *pranohara* (robber of my soul), *manoranjan* (heart's delight), *nayantara* (pupil of my eye) and *ahladey putul* (pampered doll). In the heydays of colonial rule, the British, too, were honoured, as indicated by names such as 'good morning' and 'Lord Ripon'.

Chhana-based sweets in Bengal (including both West Bengal and Bangladesh) are too numerous to enumerate in full. But some of the most famous deserve mention. Next to *sandesh*, the *rosogolla* is the best known as the representative sweet from Bengal. Its most obvious characteristic is that of being soaked in syrup (*ros*). The other is the exquisite smoothness of the *chhana*. There is no room for graininess in a good *rosogolla*. A variety referred to as the 'sponge *rosogolla*' is considered the best. Other syrup-soaked sweets made from *chhana* include *chamcham*, *pantua*, *chhanabora*, *chhanar jilipi*, *rosomundi*, *golapjaam* and *kalojaam*. Sometimes the fame of a sweet is tied to the name of a place, as in the '*kanchagolla* of Natore', the '*monda* of Muktagachha', the '*chamcham* of Tangail'. Sometimes it is the name of a shop that serves as a label of excellence, as in the *sandesh* from Bhim Chandra Nag or the *rosogolla* from K. C. Das.

One interesting point of speculation is why these sweets are rarely made at home, for the true subtlety and excellence of most Bengali foods (vegetables, legumes, fish, meat and sweets *not* made from *chhana*) is generally to be found in home cooking. According to the eminent Bangladeshi historian, the late Professor Abdur Razzaque, it was the professional sweetmakers—many of them Muslims—rather than the home cooks who were originally responsible for the creation of all these *chhana*-based sweets. This seems likely when one considers that Hindu households, with all their practices of ritual purity, might initially have resisted the invasion of the kitchen by a substance made by the Portuguese 'heathens'. It would thus be left to the professionals, working in a shop and not a home, to experiment with a new medium of gustatory delight. The practice, once started, still prevails. And capitalizing on the enduring Bengali addiction for the varied, delightful offspring of *chhana*, sweet shops flourish in every corner of a city or town in West Bengal and Bangladesh. The home cook need only step out to buy any *chhana*-based sweet s/he fancies and, therefore, has little incentive to invest time, energy and skill in making them.

The arrival of Vasco da Gama in India signalled many pivotal developments in the history of Europe and Asia, including the sad scourge of colonialism. But today, in the combined glow of a post-millennial light of enquiry, the Bengalis, at least, can savour a very special sweetness that is the gift of the Portuguese.

Food, Ritual and Art in Bengal

PARALLEL AESTHETIC VISIONS are called up by the conjunction of food and art. There are direct depictions of food in art, in painting, literature, cinema. Conversely, there is the artistry of preparing and presenting food. But all such convergence of food and art, however sublime, is about food as an object of consumption and sustenance, either in the immediate present or savoured as a memory or anticipated as a future pleasure. But there is a third dimension, where food is the medium for depicting the emotional, ceremonial and ritual universe of a people. It is a realm where, having already experienced the pleasures of preparing, presenting and partaking, one has subsequently made it into a versatile medium for both spiritual and artistic creativity, a metaphor for diverse human experiences. As in the simple and complex conjunctions of food and art among the Hindus of Bengal.

The traditional life of Bengal is rich in form, ritual and aestheticism. In sacred and secular ceremonies, Bengalis have invested food with intricate symbolic significance. An extraordinarily active folk imagination draws on food images to create verse, paintings and craft objects.

Gurusaday Dutt, a member of the Indian Civil Service in pre-independence India, wrote about his own discoveries of the entwining of art, ritual and ceremony in rural Bengal in the course of his official travels throughout the region between 1929 and 1933. He made a careful study of the artistic and musical traditions of the villages he visited—traditions that the Western-educated urban elite of that time was barely aware of and certainly did not value. And he made it his mission to preserve these traditions, support their practitioners and focus public attention on them. In the course of his observations, he realized that in this pre-eminently rural region of the Indian subcontinent, almost every aspect of life, however mundane, was an aesthetic ritual. Food, in that cultural mindset, was not only something to be consumed for survival, but also an artistic medium. It provided the raw material for painting and making offerings to the gods; it enhanced personal experience when its shape, colour and life became metaphors for human existence; it acquired symbolic meaning and enriched social customs with ceremonial value. And the creative force that was behind such transformations was a rurally derived folk imagination, not the cultivated, educated, sophisticated mindset of intellectuals.

'The most outstanding feature of the art of rural Bengal,' wrote Gurusaday Dutt, 'consists in its being synonymous with the life of the people—their beliefs and their religion, their daily activities and their seasonal and social festivities, their work and their play. The whole of life was conceived as an art and lived as an art.'

For many years after he recorded his observations, things did not change very much. Young girls in rural areas, as well as in the more traditional urban families, were painstakingly trained in the art of domestic ritual and ceremony, many of which were based on an innate respect for food—particularly the staple, rice, which had immense symbolic significance. An agrarian social structure that remained largely unchanged over the centuries, despite the larger events of history sweeping over the Indian subcontinent, created a continuous collective consciousness that is to be seen in indigenous artistic endeavours, such as the making of quilts, the decoration of homesteads, the composition of verses, the devising of innumerable rituals around the major events of life (weddings, births and deaths) and the worship of the gods. Food, whether in its raw form or modified through human preparation, runs as a constant motif through these modes of artistic expression.

A common Bengali adage refers to thirteen festivals in twelve months. Thirteen, of course, is an apocryphal number. Festive rituals abound throughout the year and vary not only from village to village but sometimes even from family to family. The festivals range from the strictly religious (the worship of specific deities in the Hindu pantheon) to the semi-sacred (the observance, usually by women, of certain auspicious days in the lunar calendar, or the practice of rituals in connection with a *brata* or undertaking/vow) to the entirely secular (weddings, birthdays, an infant's first meal of rice, etc.). On all these occasions, village homes, whether rich or poor, are decorated with intricate patterns rich in symbolism and artfulness. Traditionally, this is done by women and highlights an imagination based on an acute observation and appreciation of the natural world and its products.

Almost every visible area of the cottage—the patio, the wooden columns supporting the roof, the floor of rooms where guests and relatives will assemble, walls, alcoves as well as objects like wooden seats and large pitchers of water are decorated with patterns in a style known as *alpana* (derived from the Sanskrit *alimpana*, ornamental plastering). And the artistic medium for such patterns is the staple food of Bengal, rice. Only *atap* (non-parboiled) rice is used, usually of the short-grained variety. The rice is soaked in water to soften, then dried and ground to a fine powder which is held between the thumb and the tip of the index finger and sprinkled on the ground to create the patterns the artist has in mind. Reminiscent of the religio-artistic practices of Tibetan monks, this technique is called *gunrichitra* or *dhulichitra* (particle painting or dust painting) in Bengal. A more durable medium is created when the rice powder is mixed with water to make a thick paste. A rag, folded to form a tapering wick, is held in the hollow of the palm, its pointed end being dipped into the rice paste and used to paint the *alpana* patterns. Once dried, the patterns show up vividly white on earthen floors, wooden surfaces or terracotta objects. Occasionally, coloured dyes are added to the white rice paste.

The drawing of *alpanas* is always spontaneous. They represent a continuous tradition of artistic form and technique among the women of Bengal and the spontaneity of drawing is a crucial aspect of the art. There is no template to refer to, nor any previously documented pattern to copy—only the knowledge of patterns seen in the past and a community memory of motifs developed through the ages. Among the common motifs are the flowers, leaves, fruits and vegetables that are a part of the landscape. Ears of rice, as is only to be expected, show up often, as do rice storage containers (*dhaner morai*) as symbols of plenty. For the artist, the act of decorating a space or an object for a ceremonial purpose is vested with as much ritual significance as the eventual ceremony itself. And the choice of rice (paste) as the primary medium of painting reaffirms the importance of this crop in Bengal's life, a significance that has led to rice being considered synonymous with Lakshmi, the goddess of wealth, prosperity and grace. Even when sated, Bengalis are reluctant to waste or discard the portion of rice on their plates, lest the goddess perceive it as an insult and withdraw her favours.

Another remarkable example of the union of food and folk imagination in art can be seen in the rich and varied collection of *chharas*, songs and rhymes that are part of a long-lived oral tradition in Bengal. Only in the late nineteenth and early twentieth centuries were these rhymes collected and documented in a systematic fashion. Foremost among the rescuers of *chharas* were the poet Rabindranath Tagore and his nephew, Abanindranath Tagore. As is only to be expected, the *chharas*, even at their most fanciful or nonsensical, conjure up a faithful picture of an agrarian society where life was ritualized, expectations well-defined, the roles of men, women and children unquestioned and economic status often indicated by the food eaten every day.

The rhymes are replete with images of food, and key items recur in many forms. The region's diet includes rice (the staple), fish, vegetables and milk and milk products. As a tropical land of many rivers, blessed with fertile alluvial soil, Bengal produced all these foods in abundance, but social and economic inequalities determined the proportion of individual access. In rhyme after rhyme, food is used to depict topography and climate, the interactions between family members (one's own as well as the dreaded in-laws), prosperity or want and indoor and outdoor activities. It is not hard to imagine that women, who were in charge of the kitchen, were also the creators of these simple rhyming verses that so reflect their own concerns.

Fish and fishing are frequent themes. Many rhymes mention the son of the family (far more important than the daughter, who would, after all, merely get married and go away to her husband's house) setting off on a fishing expedition. And numerous verses have the same recurrent image of two large fish (*rui* and *catla*, both of the carp family) leaping out of the river. The arcing motion of these graceful, silver-scaled, piscine forms struck generations of Bengalis as one of the most beautiful sights in their riverine land. In one verse, the mother ponders what nourishing food to give her son before he sets out on a journey and decides it will be prawns caught from the river, cooked with the eggplant she has grown in her garden. A charming image of the close relationship between human beings and their environment occurs in another *chhara*. A young boy, trying to catch a powerful *boal*

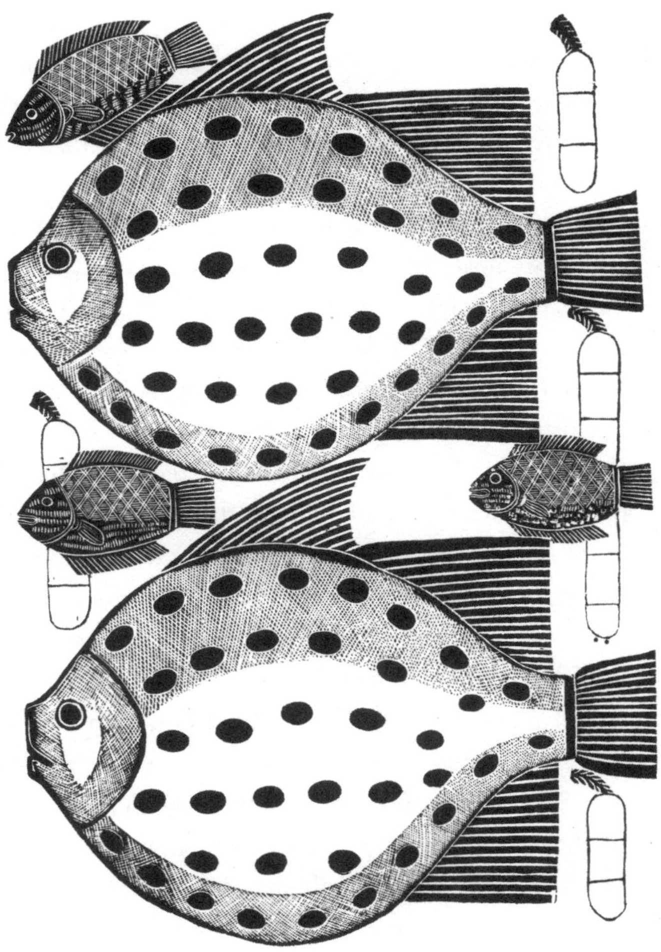

Fish swimming in water.

fish (a freshwater shark), comes to grief when the fish capsizes the boat. Disappointed, the boy comes back to the shore. This amuses an otter so much that it gleefully cavorts in the river. The boy's doting mother tells the otter to stop its antics for a moment and look towards the bank where her son, unperturbed by the loss of his boat, is dancing no less expertly. Another gem of a couplet, with an acute economy of words, evokes the image of one's dream girl whose waist is slim and supple as a *pankal* fish (swamp eel, a common food fish in rural Bengal).

Rice, the basis of almost all meals in Bengal, takes many forms. In addition to the variety and quality of rice types—according to some agricultural experts, the terrain is varied enough to grow 10,000 indigenous varieties of rice—the ways of processing rice help create a whole eating universe out of this one particular grain: puffed rice, rice flakes, popped rice (plain or coated with sugar), each with variants, depending on the strain of rice they are derived from and the way they are prepared and eaten. Rice flakes feature prominently in both the *chharas* and the folktales of Bengal because they are easy to carry for the intrepid hero setting out on his travels and because of their versatility in complementing many other foods. In the heat of a tropical summer afternoon, the flakes, soaked in cool water and accompanied by milk or yogurt, ground coconut, summer fruits like banana or mango, made a meal that was both soothing and filling. Numerous verses mention such preparations made for the visiting son-in-law (the mortal deity who held the happiness or misery of the daughter in his hands) by his attentive mother-in-law. For the traveller, rice flakes could simply be soaked in the water from a river or lake and eaten with a bit of sugar. The longer the grains and the more delicate the variety of rice, the lighter and tastier the rice flakes. In a society where the daughter-in-law was commonly victimized by her mother-in-law, many verses mention placating the latter with an array of gifts, one of them being the finest quality of flaked rice. Alas, equally numerous references to the unmitigated suffering and drudgery endured by the young bride at the hands of her mother-in-law clearly demonstrate how ineffective such gifts often were.

The cook's pride in her own art, especially in the art of preparing vegetables that the Hindu culinary tradition in Bengal is famed for, is also demonstrated in some delightful rhymes. In one verse, the speaker mentions a lightly seasoned vegetable stew of baby pumpkins or gourds—vegetables that were considered the appropriate 'cool foods' during the summer. In another, a rich merchant's daughter boasts of her special recipe for a combination dish including eggplant, green bananas, striped gourd and climbing gourd. Beyond the normal pride of a good cook, this verse also illustrates the self-confidence, bordering on arrogance, of a woman from a wealthy family. One well-known verse is about an expert cook decrying the lack of skill of a young girl called Rani, who commits the heresies of adding hot chilli peppers to *shukto*, a mildly bitter dish, and *ghee* to *ambol* (a tart sauce, often tamarind-based, and always made with pungent mustard oil). It is likely that the unfortunate Rani is being castigated by one of her in-laws who could make life miserable for a new bride with barbed comments about her lack of skills in the kitchen.

Sometimes, the cook-artist's perception of the lush vegetative world she inhabits expresses itself in innovative metaphors. Water lilies blooming in the still waters of a pond are compared to writing inscribed on paper; buds positioned around green lily pads are thought to resemble a dish of cooked greens garnished with *boris*—pellets of sun-dried legume paste. Spare, haiku-like verses evoke specific emotions simply by positioning discrete images, including those of food items, next to each other. In one such verse, a sister's longing for her absent brother is expressed through the contrast of torrential rain under an ominously black sky on the far side of a river, and a pepper plant loaded with vivid scarlet chilli peppers on the bank where she sits alone.

Perhaps the most repetitive food image in these *chharas* is that of milk and its many derivatives—yogurt, curds, whey, clotted cream, *sar* and *ghee*. Milk is an expensive commodity in modern India, something that only the well-off can afford—in marked contrast to its affordability in Europe and North America. Mothers, even the poorest of them, will do anything to give their children milk or milk products. Those who cannot are the most unfortunate of mortals. Rhyme after rhyme refers to young children, especially the favoured male child, being given bowls full of warm milk, and varied combinations of milk, rice, popped rice, bananas, mangoes, even jackfruit. In one verse, a mother calls her little boy, who answers from the kitchen garden that he is plucking greens for their midday meal. In reply, she dismisses greens as not being the right food for her beloved son, telling him instead to come inside for a meal of milk and bananas. So precious is milk that in many verses and folktales the cherished infant is referred to as a *kheerer putul* or a doll made of clotted cream. Another indication of the correlation between plentiful milk and familial prosperity is to be seen in recurring images of rivers or lakes of milk or cream. And with the facile transcendence of imagination, these same rivers are endowed with a wealth of fish which the beloved son can catch and bring home.

Sometimes humour, verging on the black, is the tool for expressing the inadequacy of the provider in getting enough milk for the family's needs. In one *chhara* a woman describes, tongue in cheek, how the one skimpy cupful of milk she has managed to buy must be stretched to cover everyone's needs. First, it will yield two kinds of cream, as well as curds and butter, to be served at lunch and dinner. Then the two older sons will get some milk to drink, while the frothing top layer from the heated milk will be reserved for the baby. A sick relative, who suffers from a chronic cough, will get his share of the miracle fluid. Nor can the pet bird be ignored—it has such a discriminating palate that it refuses to eat birdseed. And who can forget that the head of the family must be given his share? As for the lady herself, she cannot possibly eat a meal without a bit of yogurt!

The duality of milk and rice is also echoed in other widely lauded works of literature. In the

Annadamangalkabya, a long narrative poem written in 1753 by Bharatchandra Ray (court poet to Maharaja Krishnachandra of Nabadwip in Bengal), a simple ferryman, who does not get swayed from the path of virtue despite the travails of poverty and want, finally receives his reward. The goddess Annada appears before him and promises to give him all he wants. True to his character, he asks not for immense wealth but for a guarantee that his descendants will always be able to afford rice and milk. This symbol of a desire that is modest, wholesome and achievable is not generated entirely from the poet's fancy but based on a long-held regional perception about important foods.

Worshipping the numerous deities of the Hindu pantheon, those from ancient Vedic times as well as those conjured up over time by folk imagination, is part of the daily life of rural Bengal. Although the rituals, prayers and offerings can vary from one deity to the next, some elements are common to all such occasions of worship. They reveal a fertile artistic imagination, springing from the tropical lushness of the region. And food, as part of such rituals, acquires both literal and metaphorical relevance.

Lakshmi, the goddess of fortune, is one of the key figures worshipped in Bengal. Her importance, especially for women, is evident in the fact that not only is she worshipped with great pomp and ceremony on the night of the autumn full moon (every god or goddess is honoured on a particular day of the year), but also on every Thursday. Few Hindu homes in Bengal will be without a special niche or alcove in which an image or painting of the goddess is enshrined. And the weekly worship of Lakshmi demonstrates how blurred the line between art and prayer can be, and how food serves as both an artistic and a ceremonial medium. The rituals include the drawing of *alpanas* around her shrine, the symbolic offering of food for her consumption (including the essential rice as well as fruits and sweets) and the reading of a short narrative poem, the *panchali*, detailing her power and greatness. The symbolic use of rice can also be seen in the practice of filling a wicker basket with *dhan* (unhusked rice) and placing it alongside the image of the goddess. If, for some reason, the image of the goddess is absent, this basket, called *jhanpi* or *patara*, can be a substitute. And in most pictorial depictions, she appears with ears of rice in each hand.

Offerings (cooked and uncooked) made to gods and goddesses express the relevance of food in life. No puja or act of worship is complete without the making of offerings, however simple or meagre. Rice, as expected, is an integral part of such offerings. Unhusked rice and trefoil grasses (*durba*) are presented to the deities along with whole and cut fruits and other foods. The impulse of devotion is complemented with artistry. Even when a woman is worshipping the gods in the solitude of her own home, she will never set out her offerings in a slapdash fashion. Cut or peeled fruits will be arranged in circular patterns or in blocks of colour and the *dhan* and *durba* will be positioned in the middle to provide a navel-like focus. Rice pudding (*payesh*) is one of the commonest cooked items offered to the gods, combining the two universally accepted items of nourishment. Once prepared, the pudding is often decorated with *dhan* and *durba* before being offered. Worshipping the sun god (referred to as Itu puja or Ritu puja) is perhaps the best example of the ritual use of food grains. A late autumn event, the practice consists of filling an earthen pot with moist earth and five kinds of grains, including rice. A small copper pitcher, filled with water, is embedded in the centre of the pot. On every Sunday, for a whole month, women water the pot to allow the grains to germinate and sprout, and pray to the sun god. By the end of the month, when the harvest is in, they make rice pudding with the newly harvested rice, offer it to the god and, finally, immerse the pot of germinating grains in a pond or river.

The same folk imagination that devised these rituals incorporating food and worship also created the secular rituals surrounding major events like weddings, births and deaths. Food, invested with symbolism and beauty, plays a large part in some of these events. Weddings among Bengali Hindus are elaborate affairs, stretching over three days, with the preparatory rituals beginning even a week in advance. In a delta region whose rivers are prolific in fish, it is not surprising that Bengalis consider fish a symbol of plenty and use it in their wedding rituals. The Hindus of West Bengal have the custom of sending a *tatwa* or ceremonial gift presentation from the bride's family to the groom. Although the array of gifts can vary, including clothes, furniture, jewellery or sweets, the centrepiece is always a carp, decorated elaborately with oil and vermilion. The largest fish that the family can afford is acquired for this purpose and the visual totality of the apparition is stunning: gleaming, pinkish-silver scales, the dark fins and tail, the lovingly painted vermilion patterns and the background of green (the banana leaf on which the fish rests). Milk is another symbol of plenty and some families have devised a charming custom for the bride's arrival at her in-laws'. When the groom returns with her to his family home after the wedding ceremony that took place at hers, watchful eyes coordinate her first step over the threshold with the boiling over of a pot of milk. In other families, she enters holding two small live fish in her hand, which are released in the family fishpond to breed and multiply.

As expected, the role of rice is pivotal in these rituals. Apart from the *alpanas*, which are joyously painted all over the house and on the *piris* (low rectangular wooden stools) where the bridal pair will sit, rice is also used to signify the auspiciousness of the ceremony. On the night before the wedding, women in the bride's family build a small mound of rice powder (plain or dyed), called a *sree*. This is supposed to be a symbol of Lakshmi (Sree or grace being another name for her) whose favour is essential to the success of the marriage. During the actual wedding ceremony, which entails the pair having to walk seven times around a ritual fire built by a priest, popped rice is poured by them into the fire as a prayer for prosperity. The ritual of *baran*, or welcome, is performed both when the groom arrives at the bride's house and when he returns home with her after the marriage. It is strictly a women's ritual. A large brass platter, containing flowers, leaves, the obligatory *dhan* and *durba* and sometimes even small oil lamps, is held by the mother or other senior female relative and waved in circular motions in front of the groom or the married couple, to the accompaniment of ululation and the blowing of conch shells by other women. When major deities are worshipped on their annual festive days, priests welcome them with a similar ritual. Before they finally enter the house, the bridal pair is given something sweet to eat.

No discussion about the recurrence of food as both a theme and the raw material in indigenous Bengali art can be complete without a mention of the work of Bengali *patua* or illustrator. Traditionally, every village had a resident *patua* whose depiction of divine figures or scenes from myths, epics and narrative poems often adorned the walls of huts or substituted for images in the household niche reserved for worship. The illustrations were remarkable for their bold line drawings and vivid use of pure unmixed colours. The tradition of *patachitra* or *pat* (as the illustrations were called) is very old and exists throughout the Indian subcontinent. Some scholars consider the Bengali *patuas* to have been influenced by the miniature paintings that flourished under the Rajput and Mughal rulers in northern India. Whatever the influences, over the course of several centuries, they created a unique and unmistakable imprint that cannot be seen in any other region.

The preparation of paper and colour for painting shows again how integrated rice was with the expression of the artistic impulse of Bengal. Glue, prepared by boiling crushed rice, was first applied to individual sheets of paper. Ten or twelve such sheets were successively glued together to form a thick pad, which was further hardened by being pressed over a wooden board by a stone pestle applied like a rolling pin. Once the pad was dry and stiff, the *patua* could start the painting. The bold, vibrant colours used in illustrations were derived from natural substances like indigo, cinnabar, chalk, vermilion, soot from an oil lamp and burnt rice, crushed and made into a paste with water. Each of these was carefully mixed in a solution made from the gum of tamarind or a fruit called *bel*.

The subjects favoured by most rural illustrators were, as demanded by their clients, mostly sacred—scenes from the Ramayana and the Mahabharata, episodes from the life of Krishna or from the life of Sri Chaitanya. But one branch of this art shows considerable urban influence and was highly secular in content, rich in acute social commentary. This is the body of indigenous paintings known as the Kalighat pats, produced by illustrators who settled around the Kali temple in Kalighat, Calcutta. Although the temple was built in 1809, the site had been dedicated to the Goddess Kali since the fifteenth century. Rural *patuas*, looking for more work, started settling there from the middle of the eighteenth century. Most were from the district of Medinipur in Bengal. As the city of Calcutta grew under the British and its Bengali residents developed the distinct *babu* culture, the illustrators gave full play to their artistic imagination by depicting different aspects of urban life. Eventually, their work spawned the famous woodcut prints that vividly illustrated the genre of cheap romantic thrillers published by the local Battala press.

One of the best collections of Kalighat *pats* can be found in the Victoria and Albert Museum in London. During colonial rule, the paintings travelled across the oceans as part of the collections of British civil servants and missionaries. The collection in the Victoria and Albert Museum contains several *pats* which belonged to J. Lockwood Kipling, father of Rudyard and for many years Principal, Lahore School of Arts (now in Pakistan).

The Kalighat paintings project the image of a society in flux, where the men, who were in the external world, were caught between the servility demanded by their colonial masters and the libertine pursuit of sensory pleasures. Amoral attitudes and double standards were highly prevalent. On the other hand, women, imprisoned in the home, continued the rural, ritualistic traditions of their forebears. Many of these rituals involved the elaborate preparation of food and the Kalighat artists frequently focused on that. Ceremonies like *jamaishashthi* (honouring the son-in-law) or *bhaiphonta* (sisters praying for the welfare of their brothers and feeding them a special meal) are common subjects of *pats*. Inevitably, they centre on food—a large plate of rice and condiments surrounded by numerous bowls containing an array of fish, meat, legumes, vegetables, chutneys and desserts. But beyond the literal depiction lies the significance of the effort behind these elaborate, multi-course meals (the ideal feast was supposed to consist of sixty-four dishes). For the son-in-law, the effort was in the nature of a tribute—an offering made to the person who held the happiness, comfort, even the life of a beloved daughter in his hands. In the case of the brother, it was an act of appeasement—the sister praying to avert the attentions of the god of death. In a male-dominated society, a brother's death was an evil to be feared; no one cared about the sister's well-being.

Even more remarkable are the *pats* with vivid, intimate close-ups conveying specific messages. A man's hand clasps huge blue-black freshwater prawns, a medium-sized carp and a *lau* or bottle gourd. The combination of gourd and prawns, which will produce

Bhaiphonta (Brother's Day). A sister anoints a brother's forehead, praying for his welfare.

Hand with carp, fresh-water prawns and a bottle gourd.

the classic *lau-chingri*, is a commentary on the Bengali preoccupation with food—a fact well-noted in other parts of India. Another drawing, titled 'Biral Tapaswi' (the ascetic cat), shows up the hypocrisy of many urban Bengalis who hid their dissolute habits under a surface sobriety. The image is that of a cat whose forehead and nose bear the markings typical of holy ascetics who espouse a strictly vegetarian diet. But in its mouth, the cat holds a large prawn, which, obviously, it plans to devour in secrecy.

Aside from the works of illustrators, all the artistic endeavours surrounding the life and rituals of Bengal stand out in their carefree assumption of impermanence. Objects and spaces are decorated with great intensity of effort and imagination, although the artist knows that the work will vanish within days. Verses she composes will never be attributed to her and will possibly undergo subtle mutations in oral transmission. Accepting this transience as the inevitable fate of art resonates well with the choice of food items as either the raw material for art or the means of expressing—through metaphor and symbolism—the ritual significance of life. As long as the land endured, these foods would keep on being generated. That assurance was enough to stimulate the robust and prolific imagination

The Ascetic or Mendicant Cat. Of particular note are the forehead markings and the string of basilwood beads at the throat associated with the Vaishnavites.

of Bengal. Anchored in a fertile alluvial delta, nourished by the richness of its natural resources, spanning the belief systems of animism and deism, Bengal's artistry has taken the sustenance of daily living and shaped it into a medium for investing life with meaning and ceremony.

Mileposts on a Woman's Journey

MARRIAGE, considered the most important event in a woman's life through centuries of civilization, has managed to survive even in an age where traditions are vanishing at a furious clip and skepticism infuses our attitudes to many aspects of life. A *New Yorker* magazine cartoon, depicting a newly wed couple walking out of church arm in arm, casts a sarcastic light on a venerable institution. The bride, dressed in all the traditional finery of a Western wedding, carries a bouquet in her left hand, while her right hand is clasped by the groom. Friends and relations stand on both sides of their path, smiling, clapping and waving. But the expression on the bride's face, as she looks at her husband, is not one of demure gladness or romantic ecstasy. It is a mixture of relief and avidness that borders on the comedic. The caption relates her thoughts/words: 'Whew! At last I can eat!'

The bride in a traditional Bengali Hindu wedding inhabits a very different universe. Yet, she would be able to identify with this particular wedding-day sentiment, although she would not be able to express it so freely, least of all to her new husband, with whom she has little familiarity. And, in her case, food is not simply a matter of appeasing hunger after a few hours of denial. Starting from the early morning hours of the nuptial day and subsequently, at different points in her life, she undergoes a series of important transitions—as wife, mother, widow—that are underlined by special meals (or the lack thereof). The meals constitute social and religious affirmation of each of these stages in a way that is far removed from the customs of the West, even in the context of conventional church weddings. As much as rituals and *mantras*, food—offered, consumed or abstained from—defines the rites of passage in a Bengali woman's married life. In the society where she belongs, the ancient canonical rules of Hinduism and the subsequent accretions of folk belief have melded into an imaginative script where one of the basic necessities of life becomes emotive, artistic and, sadly, restrictive.

The three-day wedding ceremony that completes the Bengali woman's first major transition on the road from girlhood to womanhood is frequently punctuated by the symbolism of food, whether it is something she eats, serves or offers to the gods. The first day, in particular, is an endurance test of fasting amid feasting. The conventions of the arranged marriage (which still prevail for the majority of women) make the experience even more arduous. Long before sunrise on her wedding day, the young woman leaves her bed—whether she has had any sleep during the previous night is moot—knowing that this is something of a D-day. Her life will be radically transformed in ways she cannot yet comprehend, the agent of change being a man whom she hardly knows. As she moves around in the ghostly predawn darkness, her senses register the unfamiliar bustle that fills the home—members of her immediate and extended family already engaged in many tasks big and small that Hindu wedding rituals require. Soon it is time for her to begin her own rituals of the day—be anointed with an oil and turmeric paste, bathe, change into fresh clothes and pray to gods and ancestors for a long and happy married life. In rural homes, especially in the old days, the women of the family would go to the nearest pond or lake or river to issue a symbolic invitation to Ganga, the eponymous goddess of India's holiest river, and bring in a pitcher of water that would be sprinkled on the bride, and later, on the groom when he came for the wedding.

After her bath, the bride is ushered by these female relatives to the space that has been cleaned and made ready for the first of several significant meals that will mark the different stages of the three-day wedding ceremony. It is not a rich, elaborate, multi-course repast, the kind that will be served to wedding guests at the banquet later in the day. Instead, in most families, it is a simple breakfast, consisting of yogurt, fruits and rice flakes, with perhaps the addition of a few sweets. But it is loaded with symbolism, as even the name *dadhimangal* (unchanged from the original Sanskrit) implies, *dadhi* meaning yogurt and *mangal* meaning auspiciousness. As she eats, with her aunts, sisters and cousins blowing conch shells and ululating (both sounds intended to frighten away evil influences), the bride knows that this meal will have to sustain her through the long day until the evening's wedding ceremony is over; her relatives have already advised her to eat heartily. In the eyes of an observer, however, this ritual meal extends beyond the literal nourishment of food. It stands as the first milepost in the transformative journey the woman has now undertaken.

Coincidentally, this same combination of rice flakes, yogurt, fruits and sweets is also offered to many deities of the Hindu pantheon that Bengalis worship throughout the year; they are considered pure items, unlike fish, flesh, eggs, onion or garlic. It is therefore likely that the supposed purity of these food items lends weight to the idea that they will be enough to sustain a young woman through the hours of a day that may be apparently joyful, but is bound to create many internal anxieties and apprehensions. By consuming them at a sanctioned hour, with the accompanying prayers and rituals performed by her relatives, an ordinary human being is lifted out of her daily life and may come close to the plane inhabited by a deity. On this most significant day of her life, the woman thus verges on becoming a goddess, even though the very human consummation of the marriage at a later hour will be the ultimate affirmation of her womanhood.

Daylong fasts are hard enough for a healthy young person with natural appetites; for the Bengali bride, as the hours go by, the ordeal is intensified by the varied activities focused on food and cookery that fill the home. Late in the morning, the groom's family sends a whole array of gifts—the *tatwa*—which includes clothing, jewellery and decorative objects, but whose centrepiece happens to be an imposing carp, its head patterned with turmeric and vermilion paste, its girth encircled by a jasmine garland. The fish is a symbol of plenty, prosperity and fertility; but beyond the symbol, it is intended to be cooked and eaten for lunch by the bride's family. Aside from the carp, the *tatwa* also includes lavish supplies of sweets which assembled relatives and guests freely sample; it is one of the pleasures of a wedding in the family. Meanwhile, as morning deepens into afternoon and the kitchen emits many enticing aromas, the bride remains enclosed in her capsule of abstinence. Tradition, it seems, has determined, deliberately or not, that resisting the temptation to eat—the experience of fasting amid feasting—is the necessary tempering to which a young woman should be subjected on the day she begins the journey out of her paternal home. In a patriarchal society, marriage may promise the gratification of certain kinds of desire, but it is firmly anchored on the woman's ability to withstand desire when husband, in-laws, children and social peers expect her to do so.

In the evening, once the wedding ceremony is

under way, food assumes a different kind of significance. Instead of being a delectable concoction that tempts the human palate or nourishes the human body, it becomes a sanctified offering intended for Agni, the god of fire, who is the witness to the union of man and woman. One way of describing the married state in colloquial Bengali is *sat pakey bandha*, referring to the seven circumambulations the couple has to perform around the ritual fire that the priests have lit for them. Before that, however, bride and groom have to stand together—she in front, he behind—their hands jointly holding plates containing popped rice, fruits and sweets, all of which they pour into the fire in approved sequence. Each time food meets fire, the flames rise up in response. Participants and observers take it as a blessed sign that Agni has accepted the offering and ratified the union.

There are more rituals to follow and the Bengali bride has to wait until these have been completed before she can taste the first morsels of food. Along with the groom, she is then subjected to many playful folk customs. One of these entails the young couple feeding each other with sweets from a common plate, which necessarily includes intimate touching between hand and mouth. This is probably the most public display of eroticism permitted to a couple in orthodox Bengali society where overt physical contact between man and woman is taboo, strange though it may seem in the country that produced the *Kamasutra*. The taboos are unlikely to have existed in the early centuries of Hindu civilization when minor demonstrations of physical love did not necessarily imply shamelessness or lack of virtue. The more hegemonic, coded, patriarchal values that have been entrenched in Hindu society for more than a millennia now, resulting in an oppressive domination over women, are possibly a response to conquest by outsiders—the Muslim invaders and the European colonialists.

On the third and final day of the wedding, a very different ceremonial meal paves the way for the bride to become an accepted member of her husband's family. In the afternoon, when the day's main meal is usually eaten in Bengal, she is expected to cook and serve her in-laws a traditional meal consisting of rice, vegetables, dal and fish. If etymology is a determinant, then this meal, called *bou-bhaat*, may be considered to be the product of a rural/agricultural/folk ethos. Unlike the *dadhimangal* or the hours of fasting that follow, the two words making up *bou-bhaat*, literally translatable as bride-rice, do not evoke images of desire or deprivation or appeasement. Rather, they create a prism through which the young bride (her virginity still intact until the night to come) can be viewed as a mature, nurturing woman who can take care of her family's needs. Only after she has served her in-laws, can the bride sit down to eat. In homes that still strictly adhere to custom, this will be the first time that she eats food provided by her new family. From the previous day (when she had left her parental home with her husband and arrived at her in-laws' house) until now, she has only eaten food supplied by neighbours or friends. The midday meal completed, the bride rises, accepted and blessed, ready to begin her new life, the first step of which will be the night's consummation, the mutual consumption of man and woman.

Aside from marriage, the transformation from bride to mother is the most significant one in a woman's life in most societies. The hope and expectation of a male heir reinforces the magnitude of this step. Once again, Hindu Bengalis have used food as the ceremonial means to mark the impending birth. A very special meal, one that is solely focused on the needs and desires of the mother-to-be, heralds the new arrival. Even the name of this meal, *shadh* (literally, wish or desire), is intimately emotive. While the mystery of birth itself may be associated with darkness and secret female practices, the serving and consuming of the *shadh* towards the end of pregnancy is an occasion effulgent with light, love, cheer and hopefulness. The mother-to-be is generally sent back to her parents' home towards the end of her pregnancy in the expectation that her own mother and other female relatives will lavish far more care and tenderness on her than her in-laws can and indulge all her wishes. The *shadh* is the culmination of this caring, a compensation for the potentially life-threatening ordeal of childbirth that she will soon undergo. It is also based on the belief that a happy, satisfied mother will produce a healthy baby. Like the meal of *bou-bhaat*, *shadh* is served at midday and it consists of all the courses that constitute an ideal Bengali meal. The young woman, bathed and dressed in new clothes, often wearing new jewellery, sits down before a plate containing tasty items carefully cooked by her mother and/or other relatives. Accepting these offerings of love and hope, she transcends everyday womanhood and becomes a representation of beauty, fertility and the gratification of desire. Even more than the wedding, this is her finest hour, when she is a queen who can ask for anything she wants.

The first item to be eaten with rice will usually be *shukto*, a bitter vegetable dish that is supposed to stimulate the appetite and be beneficial to the liver. Several other vegetable dishes and dal will follow. Then will come the most important item in Bengali gastronomy—fish. Whether it is one or multiple preparations of fish, whether a fish head (the ultimate indicator of preferential treatment for the recipient) is part of the meal—all depends on family tradition and personal preference. But except for strictly vegetarian families, the *shadh* cannot be served without fish whose protean symbolism is woven through the fabric of life in Bengal. In this delta crisscrossed by a thousand rivers, fish is naturally a harbinger of fertility and prosperity. More than that, however, it is also an indicator of married bliss, the one food that a married woman, as opposed to a widow, will not do without if she can help it.

The *shadh*, like any other formal meal, ends with dessert—always a popular course in sweet-loving Bengal and the mother-to-be is naturally allowed to choose her favourites. Two items, however, are compulsory—rice pudding and sweet yogurt. Both have auspicious connotations and are frequently offered to the gods. Partaking of these substances, as in the case of the *dadhimangal* breakfast, adds an element of consecration to the satisfaction of human gustatory desire. After this, there is nothing left to do but wait—for the finality of labour, for the outcome of birth, happy or sad.

Time goes by. If destiny is kind, the years of a woman's married life are long, allowing her to see her children grow into adulthood, to marry and become parents of children themselves. Most important, a fortunate woman will predecease her husband. But there are those—too many of them in the past, given the custom of marrying off very young girls to elderly men—who face widowhood unfairly early. For the Bengali woman, the event becomes the beginning of a transition that can only end with death.

Hindu society has made food into a particularly cruel medium to underscore the permanence of the tragedy of widowhood. With the passing of her husband, the Bengali widow is sentenced to a lifetime of deprivation. In a land where geography makes fish and rice the basic meal, in a society where a woman with a husband is expected to mark that fortunate circumstance by compulsorily eating fish on the eleventh day of the moon, the widow is instantly condemned to give up fish, flesh, eggs, items like red lentils, alliums like onion and garlic, even vegetables like the green called *puin*. Enforcing and following these restrictions automatically creates a zone of separation but, unlike the *dadhimangal*, this is not a zone that elevates a human being closer to a deity; it is a zone of penance and punishment.

The period of mourning, which varies from family to family and caste to caste, is probably the last time that the widow is allowed to feel like everyone else in the family. A dead man's sons and daughters-in-law (traditionally sharing the same living quarters), along with his widow, are also subjected to the rigours of a restricted diet during these days. Cooked food is allowed only during the midday meal and consists of nothing more than rice and green plantains and perhaps a handful of dal boiled together in an earthen pot. The only seasonings permitted are a bit of *ghee* and sea salt. The evening's meal usually consists of fruit and milk. On the day of the *shraddha* (last rites), custom can be especially cruel to the widow. Many kinds of offerings are prepared for the dead—the husband who has recently departed as well as the ancestors who predeceased him. The most important of these is the *pinda*, a combination of cooked rice and fish, the two beloved Bengali staples. And it is usually the dead man's wife, who knows she will never be able to eat fish again, who has to prepare the *pinda*. In some families, however, a daughter-in-law is asked to fulfill this role and the widow is thus spared a gratuitous reminder.

It is with the feast of *niyambhanga* (literally, breaking the rules) that the entire family goes back to normal food and normal life, while the widow takes on the burden of her restricted diet and lifestyle. Tradition not only robs her of food and nutrition, it also permanently changes her appearance, forbidding all jewellery and make-up and permitting only borderless white saris. The woman who sat like a queen who could have all she desired as she enjoyed the meal of the *shadh* is thus reduced to a shadowy presence on the fringes of daily life. For the rest of the years allotted to her, she undertakes frequent ritual fasts, stays away from happy celebrations like weddings and births, and as if to atone for the unknown sins that brought on widowhood and avoid that fate in her next life, she cooks elaborate meals for brahmans and feeds them on certain ritual occasions. In a society that boasts a rich and elaborate culinary tradition, colour, fragrance, richness and taste are slowly drained from the widow's plate—a lengthy prelude to the final withdrawal from life.

The Propitiatory Meal

AT THE MOST PRIMARY LEVEL, a meal satisfies hunger. On a more elevated plane, the meal, especially if it is an elaborate offering from a master chef, is associated with gustatory delight and/or festive enjoyment. But in some cultures, the culinary effort behind a multi-course repast is intended for something greater than sensory or social pleasures. Under specific circumstances, these cultures make the meal a ritualistic tool with which to propitiate the powers that affect one's physical and spiritual well-being. The Hindus of India have used the meal in multiple ways to appease, placate and please deities, supernatural forces and human beings.

Hinduism is one of the world's oldest religions. But unlike other ancient religions—for example, Judaism—its flexible character has allowed it to acquire numerous layers of belief and practice through the thousands of years it has existed. The content of written Hindu sacred texts—unlike the Bible or the Koran—is only one part of an enormous extended system of beliefs. The vastness of the Indian subcontinent has underscored the nature of the religion and given rise to many regional variations. Thus, what devout Hindus in Bengal practise may well be quite different from what fellow Hindus practise in northern or southern regions of India. But, despite such variations and the passing of centuries, the umbilical cord connecting modern Hinduism in Bengal with its original Vedic roots, is quite evident. What may not be so clear, however, is the strong and persistent influence of an earlier faith on the formulation of Hindu ritual practices in Bengal. I am referring to the animistic beliefs of the indigenous inhabitants of eastern India (including the Bengal region) whom the Vedic Aryans eventually dominated. Bengali historians like Nihar Ranjan Ray have amassed considerable evidence pointing to this. The Hindu idea of propitiation through meals—not to be confused with the practice of offering a ritual sacrifice, which is common to many religions in ancient and modern times—very likely derives from those earlier beliefs.

One example of the survival of ancient animist customs of appeasement is the elaborate rituals performed in honour of Manasa, the snake goddess, in the second month of the rainy season. In Bengal, as in many other parts of India, snakes tended to infest the waterlogged rice fields and densely vegetated areas. One bite from a poisonous species such as the cobra and the krait could cause instant death. Villagers could only throw themselves on the mercy of the snake goddess, make offerings to her and pray for survival as they went about their necessary agricultural tasks. So great was the fear of snakes and so ingrained was the belief that feeding the creatures (as surrogates of the goddess) could ensure life and safety, that many rural households made a habit of leaving a bowl of milk out for the snake to consume on certain auspicious days of the year. The biological fact that snakes only eat rodents and other live creatures that they hunt had no effect on the persistent belief in the efficacy of the milk. In a peculiar concurrence, when a particular snake happened to make its nest near a house and yet, over time, none of the family was bitten, the popular psyche transformed the object of terror almost into a household creature. It was referred to as a *bastu shaap*, or resident snake, and a nightly ration of milk was left out for it with as much punctiliousness as if it was a pet cat.

The enormous mangrove forests of the Sunderbans area of Bengal are the domain of the fearsome Bengal tigers that often hunt man as prey, unlike tigers in other parts of India. The locals who depend on harvesting honey from the forest areas, have no option but to risk their lives as they venture ashore. Over time, however, they have endowed both the tiger and the forest itself with mythical dimensions embodied in the legend of Bon Bibi (forest goddess) and Dakkhin Rai (the tiger as god). In the story, an unscrupulous merchant propitiates the evil Dakkhin Rai by abandoning a young man called Dukhey who was a member of his ship's crew. The tiger god would feast on Dukhey and, in return, let the merchant conduct his business without interference. Dukhey is rescued from the tiger's grasp because of his heartfelt prayers to Bon Bibi and her brother who magically transport him to a safe location. The underlying belief, however, is that if a powerful predator like the tiger can be appeased with a satisfying meal (in this case, a designated human being), he may permit people to earn their livelihood.

Two aspects of life in Bengal—natural and social—have, over the years, served to bolster the concept of the meal as propitiation. Nature has endowed the region with extraordinary fertility. Rich silt deposited by the numerous rivers has made the production of food crops easy. But Nature also regularly subjects the land to the violence of floods and cyclones, which often lead to epidemics and famine. This alternative cycle of contrary events has infused daily life in Bengal with an aura of intense uncertainty. Anything that appears stable one day may vanish suddenly the next because of the wrath of Nature, leaving the hapless human deprived of even rudimentary life-support systems.

Socially, the position and role of the woman in Bengali society are integral to the notion of the propitiatory meal because in most cases such meals are offered (even prepared) by the woman of the house. As keepers of ritual tradition (religious, mythic and folk) in the home, women have meticulously handed it down to successive generations. And so strong is the process of transmission that the custom of propitiating through meals has lasted well into modern times, regardless of the numerous changes imposed on Bengali society by a series of external invading and colonizing forces. This durability can be seen in examples from both film and literature.

HINDU ORIGINS OF THE MEAL-AS-APPEASEMENT IDEA

The notion of appeasing a dangerous creature through the offering of a meal is well documented in the early Hindu religious texts. Consider one of the early stories of Creation from the *Satapatha Brahmana* (the Brahmanas were written after the Vedas and most scholars agree in dating them between 900 and 700 BC). In the beginning, there was no one but Prajapati. In his desire to create progeny, he practised asceticism for a long time. When he was almost exhausted, Agni (fire) came out of his mouth. Since he came out of his father's mouth, Agni is an eater of food. But there was no food in the universe for Prajapati's firstborn. In his ravenous hunger, Agni turned on his own father. In order not to be consumed, Prajapati desperately rubbed his hands and produced an offering of milk and clarified butter. But the offering was tainted with hair.

So Prajapati rubbed his hands again and this time he produced an absolutely pure offering of milk and butter. Agni was satisfied with this and turned away without devouring Prajapati. Milk thus became the first food for many living creatures.

One story in the Hindu epic, the Mahabharata (which scholars date between 300 BC and 300 AD), exemplifies the custom of appeasement through providing a meal. The Mahabharata chronicles the fortunes of the five Pandava brothers, who suffered years of hardship and deprivation of their share of the kingdom because of the shenanigans of their evil cousins, the sons of King Dhritarashtra.

Among the many hardships the Pandavas endured was a thirteen-year period of exile. They wandered from region to region, often spending stretches of time in the wilderness where food and shelter were hard to come by. But they had one asset for survival—a magic copper cooking pot given to them by Surya, the sun god. The condition was that as long as Draupadi, the princess married to all five brothers (an amazing example of polyandry in ancient India), did not have her meal, whatever she cooked in the pot would renew itself infinitely and feed an indefinite number of people. Each time she ate, the contents would be finished; she would have to clean the pot, put in fresh ingredients and cook a whole new meal. The pot thus gave the exiles the flexibility to feed whatever guests chanced their way at mealtimes (the forests being also the haunts of itinerant sages and ascetics), since it was customary for the woman of the house to eat after everyone else had been fed.

But disaster struck one day. The wicked cousins, who were enjoying the exiles' kingdom and wealth, heard about the magic pot and came up with a plan for further mischief. They asked the great ascetic Durbasha to visit the exiles in the forest and ask to be fed after Draupadi had eaten. Durbasha agreed to this request and arrived, with ten thousand disciples in tow, at the forest shelter where the exiles were staying. 'We are hungry,' he said, 'please give us food as soon as we come back from bathing in the river.' But Draupadi had already finished her meal for the day and the pot was empty. Even under ordinary circumstances, it was considered bad luck to turn away a hungry person who was asking for food. But in this case the problem was doubly dire because Durbasha was notorious for his violent rages and his habit of raining down curses on those who displeased him. Naturally, the denizens of whatever household, palace or ashram he chose to visit did their utmost to present him with elaborate meals to appease his hunger/anger and avoid those curses.

Panic-stricken, Draupadi called on the god Krishna and asked him for help. He appeared before her and asked her to examine the pot very carefully, in case there was even one grain of rice left in it. She found a grain of rice and a fragment of a leafy green. Krishna immediately ate those and declared that the hunger of all living beings was appeased for now. On the riverbank, the irate Durbasha and his disciples suddenly felt totally sated; they started burping, exactly as one does after a big meal. Draupadi and her five husbands were thus saved by Krishna's divine powers.

The story illustrates an article of faith among the ancients. Brahmans (including those who practised asceticism and thus became holy men) were believed to have extraordinary powers and members of all other castes—warriors (like most royalty), traders or peasants—had to please them. If a brahman appeared on your doorstep, no matter how inconvenient the hour, you had to offer him the best meal you could. Pleasing the brahman/ascetic was expected to bring good fortune; but far more important (and as Draupadi feared), *displeasing* such a person was sure to bring down destruction on the family. The presentation of a meal cooked with care was an appropriate act of submission. In Bengal, this early Aryan/Vedic concept was reinforced by the older propitiatory customs of the local inhabitants.

VOICES IN THE BAMBOO GROVES

In discussing such customs, it is worth considering the geography of Bengal. A huge delta crisscrossed by rivers big and small, bordered by the mangroves of the Sunderbans, filled with lush vegetation and dense, beast-infested wildernesses—it is a landscape that easily affects the imagination with ideas of 'other' powers. What is more, this was an area that remained primarily rural. Despite the rise and fall of major Indian kingdoms, the greater Bengal area had fewer cities than other regions. It was, in effect, the hinterland of the Aryan domain, the last wild frontier to be tamed.

In the darkness of the night, the wind circulated ghostly voices through dense bamboo groves that bordered the villages. Thickly foliaged trees cast long, mobile shadows between the burning pyres of the cremation grounds and could easily be perceived as supernatural beings waiting to get defenceless mortals in their clutches. And even human beings could be a source of menace. Practitioners of certain Bengali religious sects haunted desolate areas, on the lookout for lost and unwary persons whom they captured and used as human sacrifice. On certain moonless nights, it was believed, there was no safety even within the four walls of one's home, for these same practitioners, who were called *kapaliks* (a loose translation could be 'head-hunters'), were able to summon one from afar—a phenomenon called *nishir daak* (call of the night). Such was the power of their sorcery that the intended victim would immediately rise up from his bed like a sleep-walker and go forth to meet his doom. No wonder the prevailing consciousness was one of being hemmed in by danger on all sides. Appeasing superior powers to get protection from such perils was only a natural behavioural response. And by presenting those powers with carefully cooked meals, one was offering up a part of one's life that was sustained by eating such meals.

Death was of course the foremost and most inevitable danger. And long before the concept of reincarnation was set out in Hindu texts, the tribal inhabitants of ancient Bengal believed that the dead person's soul continued to live by latching on to a tree, a mountain, a bird or an animal. It made sense, therefore to offer food to the departed who had lost his/her human form only to become part of the surrounding natural world. One may see some similarity between this and other ancient funereal/food practices, such as the

Egyptian one of burying the dead with supplies of food and drink inside the pyramids. However, in the ancient Egyptians' world-view, those were supplies clearly meant for the afterworld. For their Bengali counterparts, the line between this world and the next was rather blurred—as if the dead refused to leave this world and the living therefore had to provide food to keep them alive.

That ancient custom of feeding the dead has survived into modern times in the form of a ritual called *pindadaan* (offering rice), which is performed by Bengali Hindus after someone dies. Literally, the *pinda* is a ball of rice mashed with some other ingredients. It is prepared (often by a man's widow) and offered, usually by the son of the dead person, to appease not only the soul of the dead but also that of all the ancestors—as if, with each death, the eternal hunger of the ancestors finds new life. And if this hunger is not satisfied, the living will surely suffer. Once this meal has been presented, the dead person's family is free to offer elaborate funereal feasts to relatives and friends and then carry on with normal life.

But it is another death ritual, which some families practise, in addition to *pindadaan* that is an even better example of the propitiatory meal. Here a mortal, a 'fallen' brahman of a sub-caste called *agradani* (literally, the first receiver), becomes the representative of the ghost of the departed. An elaborate vegetarian meal is cooked for him while he waits in a separate corner. The son or next of kin of the dead person, guided by a priest, sets out the meal in front of the *agradani* with proper rituals. Once the meal has been eaten and the *agradani* has departed from the house, the living can feel confident that the dead will not bother them—until of course the next person dies. Unlike most brahmans, who were respected and feared, the members of the *agradani* sub-caste were despised by society. Their origins lie in the distant past when some brahman was guilty of a heinous deed. Since it was unthinkable to reduce a brahman to the status of a non-brahman or an outcast, the punishment took the form of creating a sub-caste to contain the descendants of the original sinner. But the origins were never totally forgotten. So despite performing a necessary—even beneficial—function, the *agradani* brahmans evoked the same kind of revulsion and contempt that was aroused by the lower castes who burned the bodies of the dead, worked with the skin of dead animals or cleaned human wastes.

In one of the most powerful Bengali short stories of the twentieth century, the novelist Tarashankar Bandyopadhyay writes about an *agradani* brahman in a

Bengali village. The man is so wretchedly poor that he actually depends on eating as a ghost-surrogate for his own survival. When his young son, adopted by a childless landlord, dies unexpectedly, the village priest is summoned to perform the funeral rites. He assumes that in this case, a different *agradani* brahman will have to be found to eat the propitiatory meal. But the thought of missing a whole meal (made with scanty resources that the family can barely afford to spend) underscores the *agradani* father's desperate hunger. Ignoring the horror of the village, he comes forward and avidly consumes the meal intended to appease his son's ghost.

THE WOMAN IN WHITE

Feeding the brahman on specific days of the lunar calendar was also used as a means to appease the unnamed forces that brought misfortune into one's life. This was particularly the case with Bengali Hindu widows on whom society imposed the cruellest of conditions. In the old days, when women married young and were often wedded to men old enough to be their grandfathers, Bengali homes were full of widows who were little more than girls. Even when she was spared the horror of being thrust onto her husband's funeral pyre (the ancient custom of *sati*), the widow could only look forward to a life that was barely worth living. Hinduism forbade women to remarry. And the prevailing belief was that somehow a woman lost her husband through her own sins. A common Bengali term of abuse is 'husband-eater', implying that a widow had consumed the life of her husband through her own greed or ravenous desires. She had to pay for it through a lifetime of penance and hunger.

The widow, regardless of her age, was not allowed any clothes but borderless yards of white cotton (called *thaan*), nor could she wear any jewellery or make-up. Deepa Mehta's twenty-first century film *Water* depicts the centuries-old custom that condemned the Indian Hindu widow to a colourless, joyless, loveless life of deprivation. Her presence was forbidden at any auspicious celebration. Worst, she could not eat, even touch, any non-vegetarian food, which included not simply fish, meat and eggs, but also lentils, onion, garlic and even a kind of leafy green (possibly because it was commonly combined with shrimp or fish bones). In Bengal, the cruellest sanction, for widows who lived in large extended families, was imposed twice a month on the eleventh day of the moon. While women with husbands *had to* eat fish (a favourite item in the Bengali diet) on those days, widows *had to* fast. They were not permitted even a drop of water.

Even death was no guarantee of release from such misery since Hindus believed in the theory of reincarnation. Faced with the prospect of enduring a similar fate in yet another future life, the Bengali widow created her own ritual of appeasement. During the height of the tropical summer, when a waterless fast was the hardest to bear, she performed the ritual of Sabitrichaturdashi Brata (*brata* means an undertaking). An ancient tale provided the hope behind the arduous undertaking. The princess Sabitri and her husband were out in the woods one day, when he suddenly felt very tired and lay down under a tree to take a nap. She sat beside him, waiting for him to wake up. Suddenly, she saw a figure appear and proceed to extract the soul from her husband's body. She realized it was Yama, the god of death. Sabitri, however, was determined not to lose her husband. She followed Yama as he made his way to the nether world, continuously pleading with him to restore her husband to life. Eventually, Yama was so moved by her wifely devotion and her argumentative skills, that he granted her wish.

So the Bengali widow, who was so often blamed for having consumed her husband, commemorated Sabitri's victory over death with a propitiatory meal. The day she chose was in the hottest month of the year—Jaishtha (mid-May to mid-June). On the fourteenth day of the waning moon, she denied herself food and water, and spent the day cooking as elaborate a meal as she could afford to make. [The ideal Bengali meal is supposed to consist of sixty-four different dishes to accompany the rice.] In the evening, she invited a brahman to her house and served him this meal with all the grace and respect she could muster. Once he had eaten his fill, she permitted herself her first sip of water and a morsel of food.

The ritual was repeated through every year of her circumscribed life—a brutal annual endurance test in the hope of future amnesty from a cruel fate. In this instance of appeasement, the brahman, once again, is a representative of the unseen powers that rule our lives. It is a particularly significant ritual because the doom from which reprieve is sought is concerned directly with what one is allowed to eat. The propitiatory meal is expected to guarantee other, future meals for the server who faces a lifetime of deprivation in the present.

THE MALE AS GOD

The tradition of women serving the men at mealtimes continued in Bengal well into the early twentieth century, the premise being that it was unthinkable for men and women to sit and eat together. The power structure transcended class and money, being markedly similar in the homes of the landed aristocracy and in the huts of the poorest peasant. The males always ate first and were served the best of what was available. Seniority conferred additional status, the father or head of the household sometimes being served even before his sons. A very familiar image of Bengali domesticity has remained unchanged for centuries. A man is sitting on the floor before a large platter, heaped with rice and surrounded by an array of small bowls containing items like vegetables, legumes, fish, meat and desserts. A woman facing him—not quite directly, but a little to one side—gently wields a palm leaf fan to keep the flies away and to provide relief from the heat. Eagerly she watches him eat and repeatedly asks if he wants more of any dish. This is the role of the ideal wife/woman. Every day, she takes care to please the human god who controls her life by serving him the best possible meal.

Examples from art and literature testify to the length of time during which Bengali society has perpetuated the idea of the husband as god being propitiated with food by his wife as devotee. In the *Prakritapaingala*, written around 1400 AD, there is a quote from a hundred years earlier: 'A deserving man has a wife who lays out a fresh banana leaf before him and serves hot rice with ghee, *mourala* fish, fried jute greens, and a bowl of hot milk on the side.' An illustration (Plate 2) in Mrs. S. C. Belnos's 1823 opus,

Twenty-four Plates Illustrative of Hindoo and European Manners in Bengal, depicts a man (a brahman as indicated by the sacred thread around his neck) sitting under a tree outside his cottage, being offered a meal served on a large banana leaf by his wife. Her rather worshipful stance is quite noticeable. The novelist Saratchandra Chattopadhyay (1876–1938) was noted for creating heroines who gloried in serving their men food and waiting on them like devoted handmaids. Even language and idiom confirm the male's superior right to consume, not only the best of the available resources, but even his wife's body parts—*aamar matha khao* or 'eat my head' being a common phrase used by the heroines in novels by Saratchandra and other Bengali writers of the period. The woman using the phrase is usually pleading for a particular favour, reinforcing the request by her willingness to sacrifice herself.

In the 1984 film, *The Home and the World,* directed by Satyajit Ray, there is a rather ironic visual representation of the tradition of feeding the male. Nikhil, the protagonist, is a wealthy Bengali landlord who wants to modernize his household and bring his wife out into the open where she can mix freely with his male friends. But he finds nothing incongruous about the way she devotedly sits in front of him, palm leaf fan in hand, eagerly watching him eat the meal she has served. Ray shows the typical meal of a prosperous household—an enormous silver plate containing *luchis* (Bengali fried bread commonly eaten instead of rice at night), slices of fried eggplant, a portion of thick dal and some fish. Six small bowls containing other items surround the plate.

For the historian/anthropologist, such propitiation, when it is part of the daily routine, can be perceived also as a tool for clever manipulation of the powerful by the weak. Bengal's most revered writer, Rabindranath Tagore (1861–1941), whose novel was the basis of Ray's above-mentioned film, commented rather naughtily in one of his poems, 'Know that the highest seat of desire is in the tongue.' In which case, the satisfaction of one kind of desire might also be the key to the arousal of other desires where the woman may achieve some leverage and get what she wants. Tagore himself articulates this aspect of the propitiatory meal in one of his short stories, where a wife plans to overcome her husband's opposition to a girl she has selected as a daughter-in-law (marriages being arranged in traditional Bengali society) by cooking all his favourite dishes and serving them to him. The woman hopes to broach the topic at the right moment when the man is at his most malleable because of the satisfaction of gustatory desire.

A natural corollary of such domestic practice was that not only did women eat after the men had finished their meal, they also got the less preferred items of food. In most households, where means were modest, the expensive items like fish, fruits and dairy products were always reserved for men. Women compensated for poor nutrition by making deliciously spiced concoctions of the less desirable items that men would shun. The stems, leaves and even the peel of vegetables; the skin and bony portions of fish; a handful of small shrimp or tiny whole fish that could add zest to a large portion of greens or vegetables—these were the components of their daily diet along with sharp, tart pickles and chutneys. Through such denial they were reinforcing the more visible gesture of appeasement—feeding the male god's appetite.

POWER THROUGH MARRIAGE

Perhaps the most extraordinary example of a propitiatory meal in Bengal is the practice of feeding the son-in-law on a particular day each year. The almanacs, which guided the daily lives and rituals of Bengalis, assigned the sixth day of the waxing moon in the month of Jaishtha to this event. The sixth days of the moon had enormous significance in certain months of the Bengali calendar. They were dedicated to a folk goddess, Shashthi (literally, the feminine of the Sanskrit word *shashtha*, meaning six) who was the guardian of children and family. Mothers, naturally, were her primary worshippers and they honoured her on those days with the ritualized serving and eating of specific seasonal foods and abstaining from non-vegetarian food.

In setting aside a particular sixth of the moon for feeding the son-in-law, society was once again acknowledging the extraordinary powers of the male/husband over the female/wife. On this day, named *jamaishashthi* (the 'sixth' of the son-in-law) after its honouree, a human being was transformed into a deity, almost the surrogate of the goddess Shashthi, for whom the mother prepared a propitiatory meal in order to ensure the happiness of her daughter.

Several factors led to the emergence of the ritual of *jamaishashthi*. As mentioned earlier, girls were married very young. Once married, they practically became the property of the husband and his family. They had to leave their parents for good and move to the husband's home, which was often quite a distance from the paternal village. In a region full of rivers and wildernesses, travel was difficult and the likelihood of the married daughter being able to make regular visits to her parents was remote in most cases. The female in-laws of the new bride (mother and sisters of the groom) thus became the sole and absolute rulers of her fate and often treated her like a domestic slave. The husband was the only one who could intercede and save her from the more extreme forms of abuse. Naturally, a girl's parents wanted to do whatever was within their means to keep the husband well disposed towards his wife. Aside from paying him a fat dowry at the time of the wedding, they invited him every year on *jamaishashthi*, gave him gifts and served him an elaborate meal that included all the 'right' items.

One of the compulsory items for the son-in-law as god was the whole head of a *rui* fish (a Bengali carp). Even under normal circumstances, it was always the favoured male in a home (husband or son) who got the prized fish head, never the women who cooked it. But on the occasion of *jamaishashthi*, the head was reserved for the son-in-law. If the meal was not up to his tastes or his expectations, dire consequences could result. If he perceived any disregard or carelessness on the part of his in-laws, he could even send his wife back to her parents for good—an action that would lead to enormous scandal and social boycotting of the girl's family.

Two woodcut prints from Bengali almanacs (one from the late nineteenth century and the other from the early twentieth century, both published by P. M. Bagchi and Company, Calcutta) demonstrate the primacy of the son-in-law in the Bengali home. In each illustration, he is the sole male figure. He sits cross-legged on a piece of carpet (meals being traditionally eaten sitting on the floor) in front of a large plate heaped with food. A row of small bowls containing individual servings of various dishes surrounds the plate. In the earlier print, an older married woman, presumably the mother-in-law, sits facing him, obviously urging him to eat more, while two young women (possibly younger sisters-in-law) sit on either side, one of them wielding a palm-leaf fan to chase away the flies and provide relief from the heat of the summer. In the background, another woman looks on from a doorway, possibly that of the kitchen where more food is available. The later woodcut print has the same set-up, with two young women on either side of the son-in-law but the fan is held by the older woman sitting across from him. Two other women are shown bringing more plates filled with food, while another one looks on from an open doorway behind him. Only the most heartless of human deities would refuse to be appeased by such attentiveness!

A distinctive folk medium of Bengal also reflects the reality of continually appeasing the son-in-law with meals. These are *chharas* or rhyming couplets, similar to nursery rhymes, which are part of a long-

The Propitiatory Meal

Jamaishashthi (Son-in-Law's Day). From wood block preserved by P. M. Bagchi and Company established in the 1890s. The illustration seems to be from a later date.

lived oral tradition. It is believed that women composed most of the *chharas*, since they centre for the most part on domestic matters. Meals or specific food items are frequently mentioned in the *chharas* as the means of enticement and appeasement. In one example, the mother-in-law makes a long-term undertaking. She will always give her son-in-law the major portion of her rice harvest after the rice is hulled, the whole head of any fish she cuts, rice on a plate of gold, numerous bowls full of different items to eat with the rice, a wooden platform to sit on and, of course, her beloved daughter.

Sometimes, however, no inducement or appeasement was good enough. The son-in-law could find insult where none was intended and leave his in-laws' home in a huff—possibly because he did not care for his wife and this was one more way for him to hurt her feelings or show disregard for her family. One *chhara* describes such a son-in-law who refuses to eat the *jamaishashthi* meal because his in-laws have not met his expectations, despite giving him a whole boatload of paddy rice and another of the finest white, hulled rice. In the face of such churlish behaviour, a girl's parents would naturally want to get back at the son-in-law. But they would never dare, for fear of bringing retribution on the daughter's head in a society where neither divorce nor remarriage for a woman was possible. Instead, the grieving mother could only take metaphorical revenge by composing an angry and sarcastic *chhara* reducing the ritual of appeasement to nonsense. In this imaginary world where she can have autonomy over the son-in-law, she will serve him food most suited to his ungracious nature—rice accompanied by boiled *shil* (a large stone on which spices are ground), fried pieces of *nora* (a stone pestle used for the same purpose) and a spicy dish of spades!

No such obligation in marital relations applied to the groom and his family. From the beginning of the wedding negotiations, to the end of the three-day ceremony when the bride begins her life in the home of her in-laws, the gestures of giving, bending and appeasing are on one side. Even the apparently happy and festive occasion of *bou-bhaat* (a literal translation being 'bride-rice') carries a subtext of appeasement. On the third day of the wedding, the bride is expected to cook an elaborate meal for all her in-laws and serve it to them herself at lunchtime. Until the meal is over, she cannot eat a morsel that day. And without going through the backbreaking labour of preparing the meal she will not be considered a member of her husband's family, despite all the religious rites that have preceded the meal.

CONCLUSION

The Bengali Hindu traditions of appeasement through serving a meal are part of an ancient social fabric. Their origins indicate a people's intimate awareness of the physical world they inhabit, of the duality of nature as giver and destroyer and of the fundamental instability of life. The perpetuation of such traditions has resulted from the eventual extension of natural or divine powers to certain human beings—brahmans in particular and men in general. But the inner logic justifying the ritual of propitiating through meals is rooted in the perception of food and eating in far greater than biological terms. This perception is eloquently expressed in the *Taittiriya Upanishad* (the Upanishads were philosophical texts written circa 700 BC):

> For food is the chief of beings
> Hence it is called the elixir of all.
> From food do beings come to birth,
> When born, by food they grow.
> Eaten, it eats [all] beings;
> Hence it is known as food (*an-na*, 'eatable').

For those who regarded the sustenance of physical life in these metaphysical terms, what could be a better means of appeasement and propitiation than food prepared and served with devotion?

Select Bibliography

ACHAYA, K. T. *Indian Food, A Historical Companion*. Delhi: Oxford University Press, 1998.

BAHADUR, Om Lata. *The Book of Hindu Festivals and Ceremonies*. New Delhi: UBS Publishers-Distributors Ltd, 1994.

BANERJEE, Amiya Kumar. *West Bengal District Gazetteers: Hooghly*. Calcutta: Government of West Bengal, 1972.

BANERJEE, Sumanta. *The Parlour and the Streets: Elite and Popular Culture in Nineteenth-Century Calcutta*. Calcutta: Seagull Books, 1989.

BELNOS, S. C. *Twenty-four Plates Illustrative of Hindoo and European Manners in Bengal*. Calcutta, 1823 [original pages in private collection].

BIRMINGHAM, David. *A Concise History of Portugal*. Cambridge: Cambridge University Press, 1993.

CAMPBELL-PLATT, Geoffrey. *Fermented Foods of the World: A Dictionary and Guide*. London: Butterworths, 1987.

CARR, Sandy. *The Simon and Schuster Pocket Guide to Cheese*. New York: Simon and Schuster, 1981.

CHAKRABARTI, Mukundaram. *Chandimangalkabya*. Calcutta: Bharabi, 1992.

CHAKRAVARTI, Tapo Nath, *Food and Drink in Ancient Bengal*. Calcutta, 1959.

CUNNINGHAM, Sir Alexander. *Ancient Geography of India*. London: Trubner, 1871

DAS, Jnanendramohan. *Bangla Bhashar Abhidhaan*. Calcutta: Sahitya Samsad, 1986 [1st edition, Allahabad: Indian Press, 1937].

DEY, Reverend Lal Behari. *Folktales of Bengal* (Bengali translation). Calcutta: Lightnote, 2000.

DUTT, Gurusaday. *Folk Arts and Crafts of Bengal: The Collected Papers*. Calcutta: Seagull Books, 1990.

DUTTA, Bimalchandra., *Jokser Danga—A Landmark of Ancient Culture of the Yoksas of West Bengal*. Calcutta: Hindusthan Publishing Co., 1990.

GUPTA, R. P. 'Purano Kolkatar Katkhodai Chhabi'. *Amrita* (Autumn Special), 1981.

KABIRAJ, Krishnadas. *Chaitanyacharitamrita* (Atulkrishna Goswami, ed.), 4th edition. Calcutta: Bangabasi Press, 1927.

KOSAMBI, D. D. *Ancient India: A History of Its Culture and Civilization*. New York: Pantheon, 1966.

MATHERS, Powys. *The Book of Thousand Nights and One Night* (translated from the original French version by Dr. J. C. Madrus). London: Routledge, 1996.

Select Bibliography

MITRA, Sudhir Kumar. *Hooghly Jelar Itihash o Bangasamaj*, VOL. 2. Calcutta: Mitrani Prakashan, 1963.

MITRA-MAJUMDAR, Dakshhinaranjan. *Thakurmar Jhuli*. Calcutta: Mitra & Ghosh Publishers Pvt. Ltd, 1996.

MUKHOPADHYAY, Bipradas. *Mishtanno Pak*. Calcutta: Ananda Publishers, 1981 (reprint of original 1906 edition).

O'FLAHERTY, Wendy Doniger (ed.). *Hindu Myths*. London: Penguin Books, 1975.

ORTIZ, Elisabeth Lambert. *The Food of Spain and Portugal*. New York: Atheneum, 1989.

PAUL, Ashit (ed.). *Woodcut Prints of Nineteenth Century Calcutta*. Calcutta: Seagull Books, 1983.

RAY, Bharatchandra. *Annadamangalkabya* (Kartik Bhadra, ed.). Calcutta: S. Banerjee and Co., 1985.

RAY, Nihar Ranjan. *Bangalir Itihaash*, 2nd edition. Calcutta: Dey's Publishing, 1995.

SEN, Dinesh Chandra. *Brihat Banga*, 2nd edition. Calcutta: Dey's Publishing, 1999.

TAGORE, Abanindranath. *Kheerer Putul*, 12th edition. Calcutta: Ananda Publishers, 1997.

TAGORE, Rabindranath. *Galpoguchchha*. Calcutta: Visva-Bharati, 1927.

———. *Sanchaita*. Caclutta: Visva-Bharati, 1931.

—— and Abanindranath Tagore. Anathnath Das and Bishwanath Ray (eds), *Chhelebhulano Chhara*. Calcutta: Ananda Publishers, 1995.